LINCOLN CATHEDRAL is more than a building. It has witnessed over nine hundred years of worship, service and mission dedicated to God. Prayer and teaching of the Gospel, so perfectly expressed in today's choral services, can transport us in spirit to that Heavenly Jerusalem which inspired the minster's medieval builders. The Cathedral Church of the Blessed Virgin Mary, mother church of Lincoln Diocese, is a presence on the horizon visible from thirty miles away. Many feel it is like a person calling to them.

The best way for a visitor to approach the cathedral is to follow the route a medieval pilgrim would have taken, up Steep Hill. On drawing closer, you hear the bells; then, breathless after the climb, passing through Exchequergate, you suddenly see the west front and towers of the cathedral looming like a great rock face, a man-made cliff from which kestrels take flight. Considered to be the finest English Gothic cathedral, and one of the largest, Lincoln Minster is a stupendous human achievement. Yet without a desire to glorify God, it would never have been built, embellished, and maintained. Each generation leaves its stamp in some way.

It is all too easy to view the cathedral as a tourist destination or museum, and nothing more. But every aspect of the building and what has happened here – how it has been cherished and even how it has been abused – has a story to tell about humanity's relationship with God. It is a 'sermon in stone', while at the same time a living testament. Your visit will be unforgettable if you are able to attend a choral service, but even if your time here is brief, try to sit in stillness and absorb the atmosphere of peace and beauty, and let the building speak to you. If you are susceptible, you will feel you are in the presence of God.

The Cathedral Builders

The Norman Imperative: Bishop Remigius builds a new cathedral

Remigius, a Benedictine monk and supporter of William the Conqueror at the Battle of Hastings in 1066, was the first Norman bishop of the largest diocese in medieval England, extending from the Humber to the Thames. Its cathedral had been at Dorchester, near Oxford, but in 1072 William instructed that the bishopric should be moved to Lincoln, the major city in the diocese. He had already established a royal castle there, in the south-west corner of the old Roman upper city. The new cathedral was built of local oolitic limestone opposite the castle in the south-east corner.

Remigius's cathedral was only slightly narrower than today's. Its length was considerably less. East of the present organ screen, the high altar stood within a semi-circular apse, with side chapels in smaller apses on either side. The Norman cathedral had transepts, or north and south wings, and a tower over the crossing where the existing central tower is today. The nave and transepts would have had timber roofs without a stone vault, but there was probably stone vaulting in the aisles and apses of the cathedral. Remigius did not live long enough to see his cathedral completed, dying immediately before its planned consecration in May 1092. It is assumed that the ceremony took place at a later date.

Rebuilding after the fire of 1141 in the time of Bishop Alexander

It is thought that during action in the civil war between the forces of King Stephen and his cousin Matilda in 1141, or possibly earlier, the cathedral was damaged by fire. This occasioned a partial rebuilding by Alexander 'the Magnificent' (Bishop of Lincoln, 1123-48). He was a nephew of the rich and powerful Bishop Roger of Salisbury, the chief justiciar and vice-regent of King Henry I. Educated at Laon in northern France, Alexander travelled widely and was acquainted with the most advanced architecture of his day. Henry of Huntingdon, who compiled his 'History of the English' at Alexander's request, states that the bishop restored the cathedral with such subtle workmanship that it was more beautiful than before, and second to none in England. One of his improvements might have been the replacement of the wooden roof of the nave with a stone vault, and if this is true, it may have been the first example in England of a major church entirely vaulted in stone. The elaborate carving of the main portals and the frieze are believed to have been commissioned by Alexander. The blank arcading of overlapping round arches on the west front, its north and south gables, as well as the lower stages of the west towers, are all late Norman.

The earthquake of 1185 and St Hugh's Gothic cathedral

St Hugh, a Carthusian monk from Avalon, near Grenoble, was Bishop of Lincoln from 1186 to 1200. Contemporary chronicles record an earthquake the year before his enthronement. Structural damage necessitated a major rebuilding of the minster, but the earlier west front and its towers were retained. Work began in 1192 in the Gothic style, in which the pointed rather than round arch, combined with the lighter construction of the ribbed vault, and the counter-thrust afforded by the new flying buttresses, made it possible to build less massive churches, with larger window openings for stained glass. The length of the cathedral was increased by the addition of a secondary, or east transept. The new east end had the unusual design of paired chapels with apses on either side of a hexagonal chapel. It broke through the line of the old Roman wall. Hugh himself was said to have carried a hod to help with the building work, but he died in 1200, before the great transept and nave were finished. This view is an impression of the cathedral in the mid-13th century, by which time the chapter house may have been complete. Behind it, the large north-east transept chapel is believed to have been extended to accommodate pilgrims to the first shrine of St Hugh. It was returned to its supposed original proportions by James Essex in 1772.

Lincoln Cathedral with spires on all three towers, c.1400-1548

Given the experimental nature of Gothic architecture, mistakes occurred, and the central tower's collapse in 1237 or 1239 was a major setback. A new tower was started immediately. In 1255 the Dean and Chapter petitioned Henry III to allow them to take down part of the extended town wall to enlarge the cathedral. They replaced Hugh's rounded chapels with a larger and loftier square east end to provide more space for the increasing numbers of pilgrims venerating the saint's shrine. This Angel Choir was consecrated in 1280. Between 1307 and 1311 the central tower was raised to its present height. Then, around 1370 to 1400, the west towers were heightened. All three towers had spires until the central tower's spire blew down in 1548. The weight of the western towers and spires caused them to lean, and around 1730 the architect James Gibbs added cross walls for strengthening, creating a narthex within Remigius's remaining bay behind the west front. In 1775 James Essex adapted Gibbs's work to give it a more Gothic appearance when viewed from the nave. He added four spirelets and a parapet to the top of the tower. The western spires remained until 1807, when they were removed for safety reasons.

The West Front

Right: The west front before conservation. The sculptures of the Romanesque frieze were arranged in a band across the oldest part of the west front.

'Walk about Sion, and go round about her : and tell the towers thereof' (Psalm 48: 11).

The only surviving part of the first cathedral is the fortress-like centre of the west front, with the first bay of its nave and side aisles behind it. The large blocks of limestone, the round-headed recesses over the north and south main doors, and the niches either side, are all early Norman. Originally the central recess over the great west door was rounded as well, but this was raised and given a pointed arch during the building of the Gothic 'screen', a heightening and widening of the west front which was completed in the 1240s. St Hugh's statue tops the pinnacle on the south side; a copy of the Swineherd of Stow sits on the north pinnacle, blowing his horn. According to legend, this poor man gave so generously to fund the building of the cathedral that his memory is honoured here.

The west front's **Romanesque frieze [1]** was probably commissioned by Bishop Alexander in the mid-12th century. In his travels he may have seen contemporary examples of sculptural reliefs extending across the façades of some continental churches, most notably at Modena

Cathedral. The frieze at Lincoln enhances the impression that the triple-arched Norman west front might have been based on the design of a Roman triumphal arch (the term *Romanesque* means a style inspired by the art and architecture of the Romans). The frieze is a sculptural band laid out like a wordless comic strip, with Old Testament scenes to the south, or right of the great west door, and New Testament scenes to the north. The theme is the sobering story of God's covenant with his people.

During the Middle Ages very few people could read. Until the Reformation, church services and choral music were in Latin. However, homilies and sermons would be in English, and there was a rich oral tradition and knowledge of legends and the lives of the saints, which would have helped ordinary people to understand the stories told in sculpture, stained glass, painting, metalwork and textiles.

When the Romanesque sculpture was complete and brightly painted on the cathedral's west front, it must have filled the medieval pilgrim with awe for God's majesty and power. The account of human sin, God's punishment, and his promise of salvation would inspire fear and trembling in people who literally believed in the torments of hell as depicted here. Indeed, one reason for going on pilgrimage was to gain indulgences in order to remit some of the suffering in the after-life for sins committed in this life.

It is likely that the story originally began over the central portal with God's creation of the heavens and the earth, and then the creation of Adam and Eve. When the gallery of Kings was inserted in the late 14th century, these early Genesis scenes were lost. There are further gaps over the north and south Norman portals, where some panels were destroyed when large Gothic windows were inserted.

The surviving scenes start on the right-hand side of the central portal recess with the **Expulsion of Adam and Eve from Paradise**. An angel with a sword pushes Adam and Eve away from the garden of Eden as punishment for having committed the sin of disobedience to God. Ashamed of their nakedness they cover themselves with their hands. Then **Adam and Cain** are shown using tools to cultivate the soil; now all people would have to labour and toil in order to survive. The top of the next panel shows Eve reclining on a bed after the **birth of Abel,** and below, **Eve spinning and Abel herding sheep**. The panels depicting Cain's jealousy of his brother, resulting in Cain's murder of Abel, were probably over the south portal, but are now lost.

Sixteen members of **The Companie of Ringers of the Blessed Virgin Mary of Lincoln** ring the cathedral bells in St Hugh's tower. They were formed in 1612 and are the earliest known organisation of bell ringers still in existence. The **Ringers' Chapel** is not normally open, but it can be seen in the course of one of the regular roof tours.

Far left: An angel turns Adam and Eve away from Paradise (Romanesque panel before conservation).

Left: The animals leaving Noah's Ark (detail of a Romanesque panel before conservation).

The West Front

Right: ***Avarice*** *(Romanesque panel after conservation).*

Far right: A free copy in the spirit of the original now takes the place of the ***Avarice*** *panel on the west front.*

Opposite page: The beauty of the nave contrasts with the drama of the west front sculpture.

Lincoln Cathedral Works Department employs a team of experts to conserve the west front sculpture. In 1988 the Dean and Chapter held an international symposium to discuss the importance of the frieze and its urgent need for conservation. It was decided that each panel should be cleaned, and if necessary removed for treatment. At the same time the cleaning and repairing of the entire west front was begun.

The story of Noah begins on the right-hand side of the south portal recess. The haloed figure of **God tells Noah there will be a flood** to punish human wickedness. Noah immediately sets to work, building an ark to save his family, big enough to hold a male and female of every animal species. The narrative is interrupted by **Daniel in the lion's den** and then continues, out of sequence, with a delightful scene of Noah and his family still on the ark after the flood, and the **animals disembarking on dry land.** Then **God makes a promise to Noah** that there will never again be such a flood. The scene showing **the flood** is around the corner of the Norman west front, which is now indoors in the Ringers' Chapel.

The frieze on the north side of the main portal has as its theme the rewards of the good in heaven, and the punishments of the damned in hell. The story probably began over the north portal with a Last Judgement. Fragments of a Christ in Majesty relief survive in the cathedral's sculpture collection. To the right of this portal, in the recess, is the story of **Dives and Lazarus,** one of Christ's parables teaching that no matter how rich and powerful a man may be on earth, if he does not love his neighbour he will not enter heaven. Dives refused to share his food with the poor man Lazarus, and sent him outside where the dogs licked his sores. When both men died, **Lazarus went to heaven** and **Dives went to hell**, along with his two dinner companions. On the north side of the recess is **Abraham's bosom,** showing the Patriarch holding a cloth in his outstretched hands which enfolds the child-like souls of the righteous, brought to him by angels. To the left are **the Elect in Heaven,** including a mitred archbishop and a martyr holding a palm.

Around the corner, over the north niche, is **the Harrowing of Hell.** The monstrous jaws of hell are stuffed with tiny, naked souls. After his death on the Cross, Christ has come to save all the good people from Old Testament times and take them to heaven. The remaining four panels graphically describe the **Torments of the Damned in Hell.** After an **18th-century panel** comes **Avarice**, being gnawed by serpents, the purse around his neck illustrating his greed and miserliness. Then to the left is **Sodomy**, with two male figures whose hair is being pulled by a devil, and lastly **Lust,** with a man and woman having their genitals bitten by serpents.

At the time of your visit, the conservation of the frieze may be in progress. Protective wooden structures could hide from view any Romanesque panels still in their original positions. Panels which, after treatment, are considered too delicate to be retained on the west front are preserved in the sculpture collection; some of these may be on view to the public. Modern free copies, such as **Abraham's Bosom** (left) and **Avarice** (above, right) take their place.

The Nave

Reception Desk Staff welcome visitors to the cathedral. The **Volunteer Stewards** assist at services and keep the cathedral open until 20.00 hours during the summer months. **Information Desk volunteers** answer visitors' queries, and trained volunteer **Guides** give floor and roof tours of the cathedral, regularly, in season, meeting at the west end. In addition there are tours of the central tower in the summer months. (Further information and advance booking forms for floor and roof tours are available from the **Cathedral Communications Office.)**

Above right: Carved in Tournai (in what is now Belgium), the black polished marble font was imported to England in the mid-12th century, probably by Bishop Alexander. The paschal candle (to the left of the picture) is placed by the font after the feast of the Ascension until Easter Eve. It is lit for baptisms, to represent the light of faith.

'I was glad when they said unto me :
We will go into the house of the Lord.
Our feet shall stand in thy gates :
O Jerusalem' (Psalm 122: 1–2).

Space and light characterise the nave, the most public part of the cathedral, where large services, concerts and plays take place. As in the Middle Ages, the nave is used for processions, which like pilgrimages, are metaphors for the journey through life. On entering the nave a medieval pilgrim might have joined a procession; moving from west to east he would progress from the more secular to the most sacred areas, pausing to pray at some of more than twenty altars, many of which were in the nave. Mass was celebrated continuously during the morning hours. When shrines and chantries were abolished at the Reformation in the mid-16th century, the majority of these altars were swept away.

Like St Hugh's Choir, the transepts and the chapter house, the nave is Early English. This first English Gothic style of *c.*1190–1250 is characterised by lancet windows, stiff-leaf capitals and rows of dogtooth decoration (four leaves meeting in a point). The arched stone ribs standing proud of the surface of the minster's vaults act like a web holding the lighter stone infill. In the nave, non-structural decorative ribs, or tiercerons, are arranged in a star pattern, one of the earliest tierceron star vaults in England. The bosses, mostly of foliage design, disguise the sometimes awkward intersections of the ribs. Some of the original painting has been conserved, including the names of probable benefactors, such as William Paris, who was a Mayor of Lincoln when the nave was under construction.

The position of the **Romanesque font [2]** near the entrance is a reminder that Christian life begins with baptism, when the water symbolises cleansing from sin and rebirth to a new life in Christ. The winged lions, griffins (winged eagle-headed lions) and other beasts fighting each other represent the struggle between good and evil. On the north side, the two winged creatures resting their front legs on books may represent the ox of St Luke and the lion of St Mark, two of the four Gospel writers.

Off the north-west corner of the nave is the **Morning Chapel [3]**, traditionally used for morning prayer, or matins. Visitors are requested to enter quietly, as the reserved sacrament is kept here, and the chapel is used for private prayer. The main vault springs from a remarkably slender pier of clustered Purbeck marble keeled shafts. The west end of this chapel encloses the north-west corner of Remigius's cathedral; a niche formerly on the exterior of the north side of the Romanesque cathedral survives. On the opposite side of the nave from the Morning Chapel there was a south chapel, later used as a Consistory, or Church Court, where the **Minster Shop [4]** is now located.

As the Morning Chapel stands within the parish of St Mary Magdalene, the altar frontal depicts the story of the saint who washed Christ's feet with tears of remorse for her sins, then dried them with her long hair, and anointed them with oil. The tears, hair and jar of oil were embroidered on the altar frontal by Constance Howard in 1966. The design of the hassocks continues the hair theme. They were worked by the Lincolnshire Embroiderers' Guild.

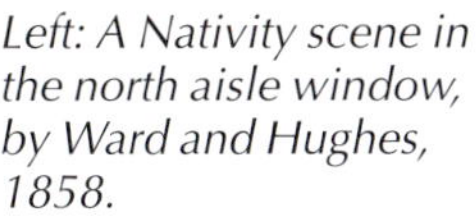

Left: A Nativity scene in the north aisle window, by Ward and Hughes, 1858.

Below (main picture): The Morning Chapel.

In the nave, near the door to the Morning Chapel, is the **monument of John Kaye (Bishop of Lincoln, 1827–53) [5]**. His effigy, carved by Richard Westmacott, Jun., rests on a Victorian Gothic base designed by G. F. Bodley. Bishop Kaye implemented reforms of the clergy of his day, such as restricting non-residence and the holding of numerous parishes and other benefices. This memorial was moved here from its former position in the south-east transept in 1953. There were once many monuments in the nave

Precious vestments and altar frontals, as well as plain linen altar cloths, suffer from wear and the ravages of time. **The Lincoln Cathedral Needlework Guild** and **the Linen Circle** are two groups of volunteers who give their skills to the repair and replacement of textiles used in the cathedral.

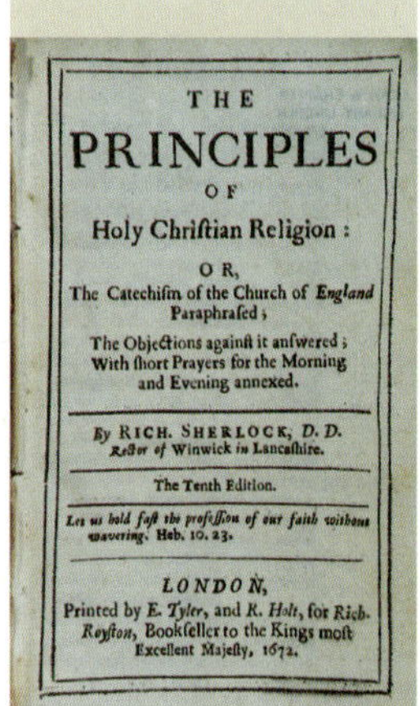

THE
PRINCIPLES
OF
Holy Chriſtian Religion:
OR,
The Catechiſm of the Church of *England* Paraphraſed;
The Objections againſt it anſwered; With ſhort Prayers for the Morning and Evening annexed.

By RICH. SHERLOCK, *D. D.* *Rector of* Winwick *in* Lancaſhire.

The Tenth Edition.

Let us hold faſt the profeſſion of our faith without wavering. Heb. 10. 23.

LONDON,
Printed by *E. Tyler*, and *R. Holt*, for *Rich. Royſton*, Bookſeller to the Kings moſt Excellent Majeſty, 1672.

Interpreting the history of the cathedral for children is the role of **CASCADE** (Cathedral and Schools Committee for the Advancement and Development of Education). Pre-booked school visits can include audio-visual presentations, activities, and tours with specially trained guides. There is an annual **Church Schools Festival**, involving a multi-media approach to education and worship in the cathedral. The children of the **Cathedral Sunday School and Crèche** participate weekly in lessons and activities which give them knowledge of the Bible, and encourage them to lead lives of faith in Christ and service to others. For adults there are a **Bible study group** and **theological lectures and seminars,** led by members of Chapter.

which, like the medieval stained glass, were damaged either by the Protestant reformers of the 16th century, or the Puritan Parliamentarians of the 17th century. Floor slabs were moved or lost when the minster was re-paved under the supervision of James Essex in the late 18th century.

Once believed to be from the tomb of Remigius, the 12th-century **Romanesque Tournai marble tomb slab [6]** under the north arcade near the crossing is now thought to be Bishop Alexander's. The Tree of Jesse shows King David holding a harp in one hand and a book of Psalms in the other. This is an unusual subject for a tomb, but it may refer to the sculpture of the Jesse Tree which was probably placed on the west front in the time of Alexander, a fragment of which survives in the sculpture collection.

Right: The great west window of 1862.

All the nave glass, except for a few fragments in the great west window, is Victorian. Lincoln Cathedral is fortunate to have such good 19th-century glass. The sun shining through the glass, spreading patterns of colour on the floor and piers of the cathedral, illustrates the Judaeo-Christian imagery concerning light as a metaphor for God, an all-pervasive presence banishing darkness and evil; the stories in the glass enlighten our ignorance.

The south aisle glass has Old Testament scenes, by various craftsmen; the north, New Testament scenes, all by the firm of Ward and Hughes. The four westernmost windows in the south aisle were made in the 1860s by the Sutton brothers, in a 13th-century style. One of these brothers, Canon F. H. Sutton, was the Rector of Brant Broughton in Lincolnshire, where he made most of the windows for the church. The Sutton brothers were also responsible for the ten Old Testament characters in the **great west window**. The **rose window** above has glass designed by John Gregory Crace, depicting Bishop Remigius holding a model of his cathedral. It was commissioned in 1858 by Charles Tennyson d'Eyncourt (uncle of the poet Alfred, Lord Tennyson), a romantic medievalist who claimed kinship with Remigius.

The Great Transept

Opposite page: View of the south transept and the Bishop's Eye from the nave.

'Be thou my strong hold, whereunto I may alway resort : thou hast promised to help me, for thou art my house of defence and my castle' (Psalm 71: 2).

The nave leads into the crossing, where the north and south transepts meet under the central tower. To the north (or left when facing the choir screen) is **the Dean's Eye rose window [7]**, and below it is the door which was used by the dean coming from his deanery. To the south is **the Bishop's Eye [8],** and near it is the Galilee Porch, which was traditionally used by the bishop when the Bishop's Palace was on this side of the cathedral. Both windows were made in the 1220s, but the Bishop's Eye was rebuilt in about 1330. The author of *The Metrical Life of St Hugh,* writing at the time when the two original round windows were being completed, refers to the meaning of their positions on the dark north side and the sunny south side of the building:

For north represents the devil, and
south the Holy Spirit and
it is in these directions that the two
Eyes look. The bishop
faces the south in order to invite in,
and the dean the north

in order to shun; the one takes care
to be saved, the other
takes care not to perish. With these
Eyes the cathedral's
face is on the watch for the
candelabra of heaven and the
darkness of Lethe (oblivion).

Of all points of the compass, the most sacred was east, pointing in the direction of Jerusalem. Sion, the Celestial City, or the Heavenly Jerusalem, were all phrases used metaphorically by medieval writers to connect churches in western Christendom with the Temple in Jerusalem, a site revered by Jews and Christians alike as the one place on earth where God's presence was strongest. The high altar is at the east end of a church, the side altars were placed on east walls, and the congregation faces east. The sun rising in the east was associated with dawn on Easter Day, when Christ rose from the dead. Burials beneath the paving were placed with their feet to the east, with the intention that on the Last Day, when they rose from their resting place, they would stand up and face their Creator and Judge. Christian burials still have this orientation today.

Appropriately the theme of the Last Judgement is expressed in the stained glass. The Dean's Eye is mostly original, and incorporates scenes which are associated with death and resurrection, such as the funeral of St Hugh, and the death of the Virgin Mary, with Christ in

Above: The Bishop's Eye window in the south transept.

The Great Transept

Majesty in the centre. Below are five lancets made up of mostly original *grisaille* (grey) glass. They have foliage patterns arranged in geometric designs, with small pieces of coloured glass. Contemporary sources describe such glass as a reflection of the varied beauty of the natural world.

In the Bishop's Eye, the graceful pattern of two leaves placed side by side in a curvilinear design was made possible by the use of bar tracery, which contrasts with the heavier plate tracery of the earlier Dean's Eye. The open stonework surrounding this window is like a filigree setting for a precious stone. The stained glass is mostly 13th-century fragments, but some 14th-century glass in its original positions appears to show scenes of the Last Judgement. Below are lancets containing medallions of 13th-century glass, taken from other, damaged windows in the cathedral and reset here in the 18th century.

The calamitous fall of the **crossing tower [9]** in 1237 or 1239 took with it part of the first bay of St Hugh's Choir, and the cathedral masons had no choice but to rebuild immediately. The lattice work of *c.*1240, which appears on the west front, is present both inside and outside on the lower stages of the tower. Undaunted, a later generation heightened the tower to 230 feet (70 metres) in 1311. The oak and lead spire doubled its height, making Lincoln Cathedral the tallest building in the world until the spire blew down in 1548. The author of *The Metrical Life of St Hugh* explains that the medieval striving for such risk-taking, dizzying heights reflects the human aspiration to spiritual heights. Listing the different parts of the cathedral he writes:

> The foundation is the body, the wall is the man,
> the roof is the spirit... The body has as its
> portion earth, the man has the clouds, the spirit
> has the stars.

The **choir screen [10]** encloses St Hugh's Choir and the sanctuary, where choral services take place. The west side, called the *pulpitum,* faces the crossing, and is renowned for its Decorated Gothic stone carving (style dating from *c.*1290–*c.* 1350), characterised by the use of ogee or double-curved arches and elaborate surface decoration. Every inch of this early 14th-century screen is carved; it is alive with tiny caricature heads of men, beasts, and fantastic creatures against a flowered background. The traces of red and blue and evidence of gilding which remain hint at a richness that is hard to imagine today.

In 1994 the **Cathedral Glaziers' Workshop** was re-developed in order to undertake more complex projects, such as the conservation of the Dean's Eye window. It is one of only a small number of workshops dedicated to the care of cathedral stained glass.

Far left: Detail of the lancet window to the far right, beneath the Bishop's Eye. At the top, Christ raises his hand in blessing; below, Moses with his staff.

Left: A detail of the 1330s pulpitum.

The Great Transept

Right: The central tower viewed from below.

The **Fabric Fund,** administered by the **Preservation Council,** continues the tradition of voluntary giving to the building works of the cathedral which began in the Middle Ages. Today, the Works Department undertakes more repair and conservation projects than new building programmes. **The Association of the Friends of Lincoln Cathedral** supports the music, liturgy and teaching of the cathedral by making grants from subscription income. Their public lecture series promotes a deeper knowledge of the life and history of Lincoln Cathedral. To foster this awareness in children, they established the **Young Friends.**

While standing in the crossing it is easy to see that the design of the cathedral is in the shape of the Cross on which Christ died. *The Metrical Life of St Hugh* tells us that in the 1220s there was a gilded image of Christ crucified (a rood) at the entrance to the choir, a reminder that through Christ's sacrifice comes salvation. Whether this was destroyed when the tower collapsed is not known; it is likely that throughout the Middle Ages there was a rood, near the crossing or on the screen, which was destroyed at the Reformation in the belief that such images were idolatrous.

The Services' Chapels in the north transept represent each of the three main branches of the armed services. The idea began with the dedication of the chapel of St George as the Regimental Chapel of the Lincolnshire Regiment in 1914. After the First World War it was decided that the chapel of the fisherman St Andrew should be dedicated as the Seamen's Chapel and the chapel of St Michael the Archangel as the Airmen's Chapel. In 1946, as a gesture of thanksgiving for the restoration of peace after the Second World War, all three chapels were refurbished and designated as Services' Memorial Chapels.

Nearest to the crossing is **the Soldiers' Chapel [11]**, which contains the Book of Memory of the 10th Foot which became the Lincolnshire Regiment and later the 2nd Battalion, the Royal Anglian Regiment. The oldest standard laid up here dates from 1685. The stained glass windows represent Old Testament figures and saints who were either soldiers themselves or martyrs in political conflicts. They were made by Archibald Nicholson in 1926. Statues of soldiers from the Middle Ages to the First World War have been inserted into the chapel's screen.

The Seamen's Chapel [12] emphasises the history of Lincolnshire's seafarers in its stained glass of 1956 by Christopher Webb. The window on the left has as its theme the early colonisation of America, showing John Smith, first president of Virginia; and also Lady Arbella Clinton Fiennes, whose wealthy family financed a fleet of ships in which she and other Puritan settlers, many from Boston in

Lincolnshire, sailed to Boston, Massachusetts. The window on the right depicts the Australian connection, featuring the botanist Sir Joseph Banks who sailed with Captain Cook, and Captain Matthew Flinders, who circumnavigated Australia in 1801. The model is of Flinders's ship, H.M.S. *Investigator*. Ships' ensigns topped by crowns indicate that a monarch presented them.

The **Airmen's Chapel [13]** displays the Books of Groups 1 and 5 Bomber Command, and 9 Training Command, with over 25,000 names of those killed in enemy action. Lincolnshire was 'Bomber County', with a total of 26 bomber airfields by the close of World War II. This chapel has some of the most impressive modern glass in the cathedral, made by Harry Stammers between 1953 and 1966. The winged warrior archangels, Uriel, Raphael, Michael and Gabriel, are compared with pilots and aircraft of World War II.

Of the three south transept chapels, the one dedicated to St Edward, or **the Works Chantry [14]**, is the most interesting from the point of view of the religious life of the cathedral. In the arched doorway of the 14th-century stone screen there are small kneeling figures, whose hands are put together in prayer. Above them is a Latin inscription which means 'Pray for the benefactors of this church.' This was one of Lincoln's oldest chantries, founded around the turn of the 12th century for the many medieval people who gave money to the Fabric, or building works of the cathedral. Other chantries were founded by individual members of wealthy families, but poor people could contribute to this fund and their souls would be prayed for by the chantry priests who said Masses here.

Opposite the south transept chapels, the scant remains of the **Shrine of John Dalderby [15]** (Bishop of Lincoln, 1300–20) can be seen. All that survives are two low shafts attached to the west wall (one with a foliage capital), and the stump of a third. Although he was never canonised, Bishop Dalderby was locally regarded as a saint, and his relics, housed in a silver reliquary, attracted pilgrims. At the Reformation such devotion was viewed as superstitious worship of the saints, and the shrine was destroyed.

Below: The Soldiers' Chapel in the north transept.

Opposite page: The south-east transept from the south choir aisle, showing the stone screen and one of the Trondheim piers.

The **monument to Edward King [16]** (Bishop of Lincoln, 1885–1910) pays tribute to a greatly loved and saintly man who was at the centre of a disagreement over how much ceremony was acceptable in the Church of England. He was tried in the Court of the Archbishop of Canterbury for certain ritual acts he performed at Communion Services, such as having lighted candles on the altar. Although he was admonished, such practices soon became widespread. This bronze statue was made by W. B. Richmond in 1913, with lettering by Eric Gill.

The South Choir Aisle and South-east Transept

Below and below right: The south choir aisle gate and detail of the hollow carving.

'I had rather be a door-keeper in the house of my God : than to dwell in the tents of ungodliness' (Psalm 84: 11).

The entries to both choir aisles were embellished with ornate doorways in the late 13th century, heavenly gates to the Angel Choir beyond, which was being built at the same time. On the right-hand capitals of the **entrance to the south choir aisle [17]**, dragons hide behind foliage, but men with swords seek them out and slay them. Opposite is a pair of owls, birds of the night, representing sinners who prefer the darkness. The medieval pilgrim would interpret these carvings as the soul's struggle with temptation, which should be put aside before continuing further on his spiritual journey.

On the left-hand side in the south choir aisle, attached to the choir screen, is the **ruined Shrine of Little St Hugh [18].** In 1255, the Jews in Lincoln were wrongfully charged with the ritual crucifixion of a young boy. The anti-Semitic hatred and hysteria aroused at this time represent one of the least

The South Choir Aisle and South-east Transept

Below: Bishop Robert Grosseteste's tomb is a modern replacement for the medieval original, which was destroyed in the 17th century. The nearby chapel, often referred to as the Grosseteste Chapel, is used regularly for said services.

creditable events in the city's history. The resulting erection of this shrine illustrates an unhappy episode in the cathedral's life. Originally there was a delicately carved stone canopy in the centre, which was destroyed by the Parliamentarians. The four **late 15th-century South German woodcarvings [19]** to the right of this shrine represent scenes from Christ's Passion.

The **south-east transept**, together with the north-east transept on the other side of St Hugh's Choir, forms the secondary or east transept. A distinctive element of the choir aisles and east transept is the **St Hugh's arcading [20]**, so called because its unique design dates from the time of St Hugh. Two rows of trefoil (three-lobed) arches overlap each other, supported on columns alternately of Alwalton and Purbeck marble and limestone. No two foliage capitals are the same. Above, between the arches, are human and angel half figures with restored heads. They continue around the walls inside the choirmen's vestry, an area which was originally open, but was later enclosed on the side facing the choir aisle by a **stone screen [21]**. Its floral diapering indicates that it is of the same period as the 1330s pulpitum, which has a smaller flowered background. Close examination of the top row reveals an upside-down comic head, and birds feeding their young.

The **Trondheim pier [22]** is one of a pair; the other is in the corresponding position in the north-east transept. The distinctive design of the core, decorated with curling leaves, was used in only one other church – Nidaros Cathedral in Trondheim, Norway. Masons' marks reveal that the same 13th-century stone masons working at Lincoln later worked at Trondheim.

Bishop Grosseteste's tomb [23] is in the far corner of the south-east transept. Robert Grosseteste (Bishop of Lincoln, 1235–53) was a famous theologian and scientist, and Chancellor of Oxford University. A slab designed by Randoll Blacking in 1953 marks where the original tomb chest was, before the chapel of St Peter and St Paul, which is now associated with education in honour of Grosseteste's scholarship.

St Hugh's Choir

Left: The choir stalls' 'misericords' are 'mercy seats', which when tipped up provided a ledge on which to rest during long services. ***The Falling Knight*** *is believed to be an allegory for pride coming before a fall.*

'O clap your hands together, all ye people : O sing unto God with the voice of melody' (Psalm 47: 1).

The choir is a church within a church, the oldest part of the Gothic cathedral, and still used for the choral worship of God. The altar now stands in the Angel Choir, but what is left of St Hugh's Choir, between the east and the great transepts, survives substantially from the earliest Gothic rebuilding.

Above is the 'crazy vault'. It is irregular, and yet organic: the first example in Europe of a tierceron vault (meaning that some of the masonry ribs are decorative rather than structural). The following extract from *The Metrical Life of St Hugh* describes the appeal of this design to the medieval mind:

The vault seems to converse with
the winged birds;
it spreads broad wings of its own,
and like a flying
creature jostles the clouds, while yet
resting upon its
solid pillars...[a work] not of art, but
of nature.

The vault has been described as a pair of scissors opening and shutting, giving a sense of movement to the choir.

Music is a theme which appears in the woodcarvings of **the choir stalls [24]** of around 1370. Seated angels carved on the choir desks play harps, pipes, a drum, and a portable organ, a link between heavenly music and the choral worship of the cathedral. The canopied and pinnacled stalls are the seats of the canons of the cathedral who make up its General Chapter. For over 900 years, the canons have been charged at their installations with the duty of reading the psalm or psalms appointed to them, the first line of which is written above each seat in gold letters. This sharing out ensures that the entire Psalter is recited every day, a remarkable chain of prayer down through the ages. The place names refer to prebendal lands from which the canons derived their income until the middle of the 19th century.

The projection supporting organ pipes over the west entrance to the choir was a Gospel Pulpit, used for chanting the Gospel and Epistle in the Middle Ages. The grey stone in the floor marked 'CANTATE HIC' (Sing here) is where members of the choir stood to sing the responses. The tradition of two choirmen standing here while intoning the Litany (a choral prayer) continued until the mid-20th century. In

At the heart of cathedral ritual is the **Choir,** traditionally composed of men and boys, with the addition of a **Girls Choir** in 1995. The **Precentor** is the residentiary canon with responsibility for music. The **Organist and Master of the Choristers** leads the Choir, with the help of the **Assistant Organist** and **Organ Scholar**. As well as singing the daily services, the Choir performs in concerts on behalf of the **Music Appeal**, which raises money from donations and events to ensure the continuation of choral worship at Lincoln Cathedral. Among many other duties supporting the smooth running of cathedral services and events, the **Vergers** carry a 'verge' or silver wand when leading cathedral dignitaries. Volunteer men and women **Servers** assist the clergy during services.

1667 the large brass eagle lectern was provided, which is still used for reading the lessons today. On top of the choir screen, a case designed by E. J. Willson for a previous organ of 1826 was adapted for use in Father Henry Willis's organ of 1898. It is considered to be one of the finest cathedral organs.

The choir stalls were extended eastwards in 1778 to provide a bishop's throne with a stall on either side on the south, and five new canopies on the north. The Victorian Gothic pulpit was designed by Sir George Gilbert Scott in 1863–4. In 1892–3 statues of saints and English royalty were placed in the canopies of the choir stalls, and repairs and additions were made.

The **sanctuary [25]** where the high altar is situated was very different in the 17th century, when it was furnished with panelling. A simple table replaced the altar, reflecting the thinking that a table, not an altar, was used at the Last Supper, which is commemorated at the Communion Service. But in 1769, at the Dean and Chapter's request, the cathedral architect James Essex recreated a Gothic sanctuary by reinstating the stone choir screen, and adding a stone reredos behind the altar, which was based on the *c.*1300 tomb of Bishop de Luda at Ely Cathedral. The centre first held a painting of St Peter in Chains, replaced in 1799 by a painting of the Annunciation (when Mary learned she was to be the mother of Christ). This, too, was removed and now hangs in the north-east transept. More Gothic detail was added in the 19th century, and the upper part was pierced, affording a view of the great east window. Sunday Communion is currently celebrated on a table placed in front of the high altar, a practice which allows the priest to face the people.

The three canopied niches on the left are part of the *c.*1300 sepulchre, traditionally believed to be the **tomb of Remigius [26a].** Appropriately for the founder of the cathedral, his remains were placed in the most sacred area by the high altar and next to the Easter Sepulchre, or more precisely, **the Tomb of Christ [26b].** The reliefs of three chain-mailed sleeping knights at the bottom represent the soldiers who guarded Christ's tomb. It is thought that before the Reformation this structure had a ceremonial use during Holy Week. It may also have served as a sacrament shrine, where the consecrated

Opposite page: St Hugh's Choir, looking west.
Above: The 1698 brass chandelier.
Below: The Tomb of Christ and the paschal candle.

St Hugh's Choir

host was reserved. In observance of a medieval tradition, the paschal candle is lit here for the forty days between Easter and the Ascension, marking the period when the risen Christ, in his own words, 'the light of the world', appeared on numerous occasions to his disciples before ascending to heaven.

The chantry chapel of Katherine Swynford [27] is the burial place of the woman who was first the mistress and then the wife of one of the richest and most powerful men in Plantagenet England. John of Gaunt (son of Edward III), Duke of Lancaster and Earl of Lincoln, was not free to marry her until 1396 when his wife died, by which time the couple already had four children who bore the name of Beaufort. Their births were legitimised retrospectively after their parents' wedding in Lincoln Cathedral. One of their descendants, Lady Margaret Beaufort, was the mother of Henry VII. Masses were said here for the souls of Katherine and her family until the Reformation. The smaller tomb of Joan Beaufort, Countess of Westmorland, once lay beside her mother's.

Opposite page: The high altar is in the sanctuary. This area was rebuilt in the late 13th century to form part of the Angel Choir.

Far left: The tomb of Katherine Swynford.

Left: The clergy, choir and servers say a prayer in the south-east transept before processing to St Hugh's Choir for Sunday Eucharist.

The Angel Choir

'Praise him in the sound of the trumpet : praise him upon the lute and harp'
(Psalm 150: 3).

St Hugh was canonised in 1220, twenty years after his death. His cult became so popular that in 1255 it was decided to extend the east end to provide more space for pilgrims, as well as new north and south entrances. (To view the **Judgement Porch [38]**, walk round the outside of the building on the south side.) The black lines on the floor mark where the foundations of St Hugh's short-lived east end were discovered. The Angel Choir was built during the Geometric period of Gothic architecture (*c.*1255–90), characterised by more complex 'geometric' window designs and naturalistic carving.

On 6 October 1280, enough of the Angel Choir was complete to allow the ceremony of the translation, or re-siting, of St Hugh's remains, witnessed by King Edward I and Queen Eleanor. Nothing is now left of the shrine destroyed at the Reformation, which is thought to have been raised up east of the choir screen and surrounded by railings. In around 1330 a separate shrine was made for the relic of the head of St Hugh.

The head shrine of St Hugh [28a] is the base for what was probably a portable shrine (now lost), which could be carried in processions. It was not unusual in the Middle Ages for various bones to be removed from the body of a saint to be venerated separately, taken to the sick, or

Above: A roof boss in the south aisle of a princess with two puppies and a page.
Below: St Hugh's head shrine with its reliquary, from Dugdale's ***Book of Monuments.***
Opposite page: The Angel Choir, looking towards the head shrine base.

given to other churches. Providing a secondary shrine made access easier for the numerous pilgrims. Those seeking miracles would try to get as close as possible, sitting in the niches and touching the stone. They would remain there night and day, praying and waiting. Thank-offerings for favours granted would abound, often in the form of candles to match the height of the person who credited his recovery from an illness to the intercession of the saint. A clerk would record miracles and watchmen slept in the cathedral in order to guard the relics.

In 1986, to celebrate the 800th year of St Hugh's arrival in Lincoln, the jeweller and sculptor David Poston was commissioned by the Dean and Chapter to design a canopy for the head shrine base, made of bronze-coated stainless steel. Its curving lines are like the back and neck of the tame swan which used to greet St Hugh when he approached his manor at Stow Park.

The Angel Choir sculpture shows a progression eastward from earthly life through death to salvation and eternal life in heaven. High between the triforium gallery arches, an angel with a sword turns Adam and Eve away from the Garden of Eden for their sin. Christ's death on the Cross to redeem sinners is portrayed by the wounded Christ, and nearby angels proudly display the nails, crown of thorns, and other instruments of his Passion. The Last Judgement is referred to by an angel holding scales: if a soul's worth is out-weighed by his unrepented sins he will not enter the kingdom of heaven. Beyond in the retrochoir, heavenly angel musicians play trumpets, a viol, a harp, a pipe and a drum. Other angels carry scrolls, which may have had inscriptions on them when the sculptures were first painted.

It has been suggested that the Angel Choir was inspired by the 'Laudate Psalms' (Psalms 148 to 150), which have as their theme a joyous praising of God. In Psalm 148, young men and maidens, old men and children praise the Lord, like the great company of people whose heads are carved between the arches of the arcade, and in the blank arcading of the outer walls. Psalm 149, verses 5–9, speaks of the saints praising God, rejoicing in their beds; the tomb in which St Hugh's body rested would have been the focal point of the Angel Choir. On the south side, King David, the author of the psalms, is

Above: An angel holding the sun and moon in the Angel Choir north triforium gallery. Note the face of the man in the moon.

Below right: The Lincoln Imp.

portrayed with wings, playing his harp and looking towards the **great east window [28b]** of *c.*1275. This is the first Gothic eight-light window, the size of which must have been a marvel in its day (59 feet, or 18 metres in height). In the Middle Ages the office of Lauds, including the Laudate Psalms, would have been sung at dawn, when the rising sun would represent Christ's rising from the dead on Easter morning. Light shining through the (now lost) medieval glass of this window would pass over the smiling faces of the angels. One angel nearby on the north side holds the sun in one hand and the moon in the other, as in Psalm 148, verses 2 to 3:

> Praise him, all ye angels of his :
> praise him, all his host.
> Praise him, sun and moon : praise
> him, all ye stars and light.

The effect would have been at once ephemeral and eternal. Earthly joys are as fleeting as a sunbeam, yet in heaven praise and joy are unceasing.

On a sacramental level, in the triforium sculpture near the high altar on the north side, Christ points to the wound in his side, signifying the Blood of Christ in the Eucharist. An angel presents the small figure of a soul to him, an allegory for the soul's need for spiritual food. Reinforcing the theme is an angel with a hawk and a piece of meat. The hawk flies away, but is lured back by its hunger, as the human soul is tempted to turn away from God, but is drawn back to feed on Christ in Communion.

The well-known **Lincoln Imp [29]** can be found above the pier closest to the head shrine. A man's head is set between

The Angel Choir

Left: Christ wearing the Crown of Thorns. This and other Angel Choir figures can be found between the arches of the triforium galleries, above the piers of the arcades and below the clerestory windows.

the arches springing from the capitals at the top of the pier; above is a little devil with horns and claws, covered in feathers, nonchalantly crossing his leg. Legend has it that he was once alive, but owing to the havoc he caused he was turned to stone by the angels. The local jeweller James Usher made a fortune from selling souvenir reproductions of the Lincoln Imp in gold and silver. The money he left to the City Council financed the building of the Usher Gallery.

Below and to the right of the great east window, with its 1855 Ward and Hughes stained glass showing the life of Christ with related Old Testament salvation stories, is **Eleanor of Castile's visceral tomb [30].** Ten years after attending the dedication of the Angel Choir, Queen Eleanor died in Harby, near Lincoln. Her distraught husband had her viscera interred at Lincoln, and on each stop along their route to London he instructed a cross to be erected, beginning at Cross o' Cliff hill in Lincoln and ending at Charing Cross. Her heart was buried in Blackfriars in London, and her body rests in a tomb at Westminster Abbey. To mark the six hundredth anniversary of Eleanor's death, her monument was restored in 1890. The base is a copy of the original, and the effigy is a replica of the medieval bronze figure by William Torel on Eleanor's tomb in Westminster Abbey.

The **cathedral flower arrangers** give of their time, skills, and flowers from their own gardens, to enhance the beauty of the building with offerings from the natural world.

The Angel Choir Chantry Chapels

There are five Angel Choir chantry chapels of which some evidence survives. No longer dedicated to prayers for the souls of dead founders, the Longland, Russell and Fleming chapels are used today for said (rather than sung) week-day services. A lit candle outside the door of these, and other chapels in the great transept, indicates when a service is in progress.

Henry VIII's confessor, John Longland (Bishop of Lincoln, 1521–47), built this chantry chapel in preparation for his own death. What is known as **Bishop Longland's Chantry [31]** was never founded, because by the time he died chantries were illegal. This chapel is used for private prayer. Cards requesting prayers can be written and left here to be read and placed on the high altar at Sunday Eucharist.

The **Russell Chantry [32]**, like the Longland Chantry, is a small Perpendicular (late Gothic, *c.*1335–50 to *c.*1530) annex with the tomb chest placed in the wall of the cathedral under a niche. John Russell (Bishop of Lincoln, 1483–94) was Lord Chancellor to Richard III. The **altar and wall paintings by Duncan Grant** date from 1958, and reflect the chapel's dedication to St Blaise, patron saint of woolcombers. The east wall shows Christ the Good Shepherd; on the opposite wall is the loading of wool on to ships in medieval Lincoln.

Next to the Russell Chantry is the **Cantilupe Chantry [33]**, where there are two tombs which suffered damage by the Parliamentarians. The altar dedicated to St Nicholas would originally have been under the south choir aisle east window, which includes a scene from the life of St Nicholas, among other 13th-century roundels reset here from damaged windows. When John Leland visited sometime between 1535 and 1543, he records having seen in this chapel 'a merveylows fair and large Psalter, full in the margin of goodly armes of many noble men'. All of the Lincoln service books and music manuscripts were destroyed at the

Below left: The Longland Chantry.

Below right: The Burghersh Chantry. In 1984 large pottery candlesticks by Robin Welch were dedicated to Gilbert of Sempringham, an older contemporary of St Hugh and a native of Lincolnshire. His Gilbertine Order was the only medieval monastic order founded in England. This is an informal area where people light candles and say a prayer or reflect.

Above: Detail of the east window of the south choir aisle, in the Cantilupe Chantry, showing Noah in the Ark receiving the dove.

Reformation; the only surviving fragments were reused in later bindings.

Both the Cantilupe Chantry and the **Burghersh Chantry [34a]** at the east end of the north choir aisle were separated from the central east end chapel in the Middle Ages by screens and high stone canopies over the tombs. Much of the reset 13th-century glass of the **Theophilus window [34b]** tells the story of a man who sold his soul to the devil (portrayed here with a red face), but later repented and was saved. The chantry was founded in 1348/9 for the souls of the family of Bartholomew Burghersh, a baron whose tomb is against the north wall; his brother Henry Burghersh (Bishop of Lincoln, 1320–40) has his monument behind the head shrine. As well as providing a priest to offer Mass for the souls of the dead, this foundation also paid for the maintenance and education of six boys. When the chantry was dissolved the endowment was transferred to the cathedral choir. All but four of the boy choristers are still referred to as 'Burghersh Chanters'.

The **Fleming Chantry [35]**, annexed to the north wall near the Gilbert Pots, was founded by Robert Fleming (Dean of Lincoln, 1452–83) for his own soul and that of his uncle, Richard Fleming (Bishop of Lincoln, 1420–31). The bishop's effigy

Right: The Judgement Porch tympanum before restoration. Entering the Angel Choir through this porch, the medieval pilgrim would see above the door the Day of Judgement, contrasted with the joys of heaven to be found in the Angel Choir beyond. On the left, angels guide the good to Paradise; on the right, devils stuff the damned into hell.

Duty chaplains are clergy and Readers who volunteer from Easter to early October to give a day in rotation in order to respond to visitors' spiritual needs. The Vergers also help to ensure that anyone in need of advice or consolation who enters the cathedral should feel welcome. In response to requests for prayer, the **Remigius Group** prays for individuals and their problems. There is also an **Intercessory Prayer Group**, which meets regularly.

in life is contrasted with an image of his body decaying in his shroud below. It is the earliest example in England of this type of reminder that in death all pomp and show is gone.

Two prominent 19th-century churchmen have monuments in the Angel Choir, east of the choir screen. **Christopher Wordsworth [36]** (Bishop of Lincoln, 1869–85), a nephew of the poet, is represented lying under a Victorian Gothic canopy, wearing a mitre, although he was never known to wear a mitre in life. He founded Lincoln Theological College, which flourished for over a hundred years. The other monument with an effigy is that of **William Butler [37]** (Dean of Lincoln, 1885–94). While Vicar of Wantage he founded the Community of St Mary the Virgin, an order of Anglican nuns. They embroidered a magnificent altar frontal for the high altar enlarged by Dean Butler, which is still used on Easter Day.

The North-east Transept

'For I love thy commandments : above gold and precious stone'
(Psalm 119: 127).

A prominent feature of the north-east transept is the **wall painting of four early bishops of Lincoln by the Venetian Vincenzo Damini [39a]**, which was painted over a medieval wall painting of the same subject in 1728. Bishops Robert Bloet, Alexander, Robert de Chesney and Walter of Coutances were traditionally believed to be buried in this transept. Beneath the wall painting is a **reset door**

Right: A detail of the medieval ironwork.

The North-east Transept

with scrolling medieval ironwork [39b].

Iron grilles of 1297 [40] divide the north- and south-east transepts from St Hugh's Choir. As elsewhere in the cathedral, the floor bears the impressions of brasses. John Evelyn records in his diary in 1654 the devastation caused by Cromwell's forces during the previous decade: '..the Souldiers ... went in with axes & hammers, & shut themselves in, till they had rent & torn of[f] some barges of Mettal; not sparing the monuments of the dead, so hellish an avarice possess'd them.'

The Treasury [41] provides a secure place to display silver chalices and other plate from churches in the diocese, as well as some personal plate retrieved from burials of medieval bishops of Lincoln – some of the few precious items which were not taken by Henry VIII's commissioners and sent to the Tower of London.

On the way to the cloister is a **tactile display for the blind,** including materials which visitors can freely touch, such as lead, stone, and timber.

The Treasury was established in 1960 with the help of the Goldsmiths' Company. Its design is by Louis Osman, with glass by Geoffrey Clarke. The ***Custos Thesauri,*** a curator, oversees volunteer **Treasury stewards.**

Left: At the junction of the north choir aisle and north-east transept is the second of the two Trondheim piers. It stands at the corner of the Treasury.

The Cloister and Chapter House

Right: The cloister from the north-west.

Below right: A hare among the cloister bosses.

Below, far right: The Virgin and Child, with the Holy Spirit represented by a dove.

Opposite page: Exterior of the chapter house.

The **Chapter** are residentiary canons who are responsible along with the **Chapter Clerk** for the administration of the cathedral and its employees; and also for cathedral worship and various other activities, on both a local and diocesan level. Non-voting **members of Chapter**, both lay and ordained, attend Chapter meetings in an advisory capacity. The **Dean** has particular responsibility for the cathedral; both he and the **Subdean** are Masters of the Fabric. The **Lincoln Cathedral Community Association** represents those who worship, work, and serve in the cathedral.

'Peace be within thy walls : and plenteousness within thy palaces' (Psalm 122:7).

The cloister and chapter house are approached from the north-east transept through a vaulted passage called the **slype [42].** Both here and in the cloister, the bosses are of superb quality. The cloister bosses are unusual because they, like the vaults, are wooden. The Man with the Toothache in the south walk, the Lion Head in the west walk, and the Virgin and Child in the east walk, are all well worth spending some time to find.

The term 'minster' indicates a large church served by clergy who were not living a monastic life, and this was the case at Lincoln, which is both a minster and a cathedral. Although many medieval canons had houses in Minster Yard, they often appointed vicars to fulfil their liturgical duties in the cathedral, so that they lived for most of the year elsewhere, perhaps in a parish, or a house connected

The Cloister and Chapter House

with some other benefice. Strictly speaking, **the cloister [43]** was not required. It may be an example of the desire to offer the very best and most complete in building to the greater glory of God. In *c.*1153 the French theologian Hugh of Fouilly wrote a treatise called 'On the monastery of the soul', in which he describes the cloister in contemplative terms, likening each side to different aspects of meditation on heavenly things: contempt for self, contempt for the world, love of God and love of one's neighbour. Canons, chantry priests, vicars, choristers, and all involved in daily cathedral worship in the Middle Ages must have found peace enjoying the cloister garden, or benefiting from exercise in inclement weather before their next cathedral duty.

During extensive repairs between 1888 and 1892, the architect J. L. Pearson discovered some early 13th-century blank arcading on either side of the entrance to the chapter house, which had been walled over when the cloister was built (from *c.*1295). A fragment of the original work survives in the corner, to the left of the door leading to the cathedral. Pearson restored this series of arches with funds raised by an appeal.

The ten-sided **chapter house [44],** begun in the 1220s, is still used for meetings of the General Chapter who traditionally sit on the stone seats which are let into the walls. The slender ten-sided central pier supports twenty stone ribs, which fan out into a tierceron vault. Eight flying buttresses and pinnacles make a counter-weight to the enormous thrust of the vault and roof above. Edward I called one of the earliest English Parliaments here in 1301; in 1536 the leaders of the Lincolnshire Rising, who resisted the Reformation, gathered here to receive Henry VIII's reply to their demands. The late 19th-century stained glass windows by Clayton and Bell trace the history of the cathedral from William the Conqueror to John Wesley's last visit in 1790. The canopied chair is said to date from *c.*1300.

The Library

Below right: A wedding from a c. 1400 manuscript in the Cathedral Library's collection.

Opposite page: The Wren Library.

Group visits can be arranged to both the Medieval and Wren Libraries. The reading room is open by appointment to readers wishing to consult the reference collection there, or the rare books kept in the Wren Library. In addition there are annual events including lectures, concerts and readings. The **Library volunteers** steward exhibitions, index, help with clerical work, and refurbish books under the supervision of the **Librarian.** The member of Chapter who has responsibility for the library and education is the **Chancellor.**

'Thou, O God, hast taught me from my youth up until now : therefore will I tell of thy wondrous works.
Forsake me not, O God, in mine old age, when I am gray-headed: until I have shewed thy strength unto this generation, and thy power to all them that are yet for to come' (Psalm 71: 15–16).

Michael Honywood was appointed Dean at the restoration of the monarchy in 1660. Cathedral chapters

and choirs had been abolished since 1643, and the damage to the fabric of the cathedral was enormous. Honywood's great legacy to Lincoln Cathedral was his gift of the **Wren Library [45]**. In 1674 he chose the famous English Baroque architect, Sir Christopher Wren, who designed the new building over an open loggia, or walkway, on the site of the then ruinous north range of the cloister. Honywood bequeathed his vast library of around 5000 books, on a wide range of subjects, to add to the 100 medieval manuscripts already in the possession of the cathedral, which were kept chained to the oak desks in the *c.*1422 **Medieval Library[46]**. This earlier building had originally extended south towards the chapter house, but nearly half of it was lost in a fire, the date of which was not recorded. It is known that repairs were carried out in 1789, when the truncated exterior of the Medieval Library was faced in ashlar masonry in order to make it blend in with the Wren Library. Its roof retains mostly original timbers, bosses, and carved angels. This room is used for annual exhibitions, usually about some aspect of church history, based on the books and manuscripts from the library's collection and the Dean and Chapter archives.

For further information:

A History of Lincoln Minster, edited by Dorothy Owen (Cambridge University Press, 1994), is a collection of essays on the cathedral's history, architecture and music. Information on art and architecture can be found in *The Buildings of England: Lincolnshire*, Nikolaus Pevsner and John Harris (2nd ed. revised by Nicholas Antram, Penguin, 1989); *The British Architectural Association Conference Transactions for the Year 1982, VII: Medieval Art and Architecture at Lincoln Cathedral*, edited by T. A. Heslop and V. A. Sekules, 1986; *The Romanesque Frieze and its Spectator*, edited by D. A. Kahn, 1992. Paul Binski's paper on the interpretation of the Angel Choir appears in *Art History*, vol. 20/3, 1997.

Three books among a number of Cathedral publications on sculpture are George Zarnecki's *Romanesque Lincoln*, 1988; C. R. Brighton's *Lincoln Cathedral Cloister Bosses*, 1985; and Lynne Broughton's *Interpreting Lincoln Cathedral*, 1996. *The Metrical Life of St Hugh*, trans. Charles Garton, is quoted in the text. Lincoln Cathedral Publications include biographies, sermons and lectures, and are on sale in the Minster Shop.

Queries concerning visits, volunteering, and joining in activities and associations can be answered by staff in the **Communications Office** (telephone: 01522 544544).

Text: Carol Bennett · Drawings: David Vale · Photography: Elizabeth Nye Carpenter, all rights reserved · Photograph of the West Front before conservation by Judges Postcards Ltd · Additional photographs by Nicholas Bennett; Susan Friend; Heather Lees; the Cathedral Works Department · Design: Max Marschner, Ampersand Designs, Lincoln · Typesetting: Elizabeth Nurser, Yard Publishing Services, Sudbury · Printed by G. W. Belton Ltd, Gainsborough · Published by Lincoln Cathedral Publications ·

ISBN 1 870561 13 9